Bristol Radical Pa

Indoctrinating for Empire

Children's books and changing times

Colin Thomas

ISBN 978-1-911522-63-8

Bristol Radical History Group. 2022.
www.brh.org.uk
brh@brh.org.uk

During the coronavirus lockdown Bristol Refugee Rights decided to keep in touch with the children of refugees and asylum seekers by organising weekly on-line story-telling sessions. I was given the difficult job of choosing and reading those stories—so many of those in the bookshops assumed a comfortable white middle-class background like the one I had come from. It made me realize how much I had once been influenced by the books I had grown up with, books of fiction as much as those purporting to be factual accounts of British history.

When I was at school, seadogs like Sir John Hawkins and Sir Francis Drake were still seen as part of a long line of British heroes. As late as 1955, historian Geoffrey Elton in his best-selling *England Under the Tudors* wrote of Hawkins as "one of the founding fathers of England's naval tradition ... he was a man of commanding presence and intellect, of outstanding abilities as a seaman, administrator, fighter and diplomat, and endowed with such charm that even his opponents in the Spanish colonies could only remark ruefully that, once you let Hawkins talk to you, you would end up doing his will."

His African victims found him less charming—Hawkins was the founder of the British slave trade. Learning that a "store of Negroes might easily be had upon the coast of Guinea", he resolved "to make trial thereof".[1] In 1562 he sailed to the River Sierra Leone and captured 300 Africans partly, as he said, "by the sword and partly by other means." The other means included seizing slaves from Portuguese traders.[2] Hawkins then sold them to Spanish plantation owners in the West Indies. His three voyages to the Caribbean in the 1560s, one of them with Drake, were primarily slaving voyages.[3]

In order to justify the horrors that slave traders were inflicting on their cargoes, they and their apologists developed the idea of a racial hierarchy, with Africans seen as a lower order of humanity. "A parcel of creatures nastier than swines",[4] wrote slave captain Thomas Phillips of his cargo, and theologians sought a bizarre explanation through a notion that black people were descended from Ham, a son of Noah who Noah had cursed.

"As [the] British empire grew and peaked in the nineteenth and twentieth century," writes Sathnam Sanghera, "it morphed into nothing less than a wilful, unapologetic exercise in white racial supremacy".[5] In the early years of British rule in India, there was a degree of cross-cultural mixing and marriages between the British and Indians but "the rise of the Victorian Evangelicals in

1 Quoted by Hugh Thomas in *The Slave Trade* (London, Papermac, 1997) 155
2 Hugh Thomas, 156
3 Hugh Thomas, 12
4 Quoted by Chris Evans in *Slave Wales* (Cardiff, University of Wales Press, 2010) 27
5 Sathnam Sanghera *Empireland* (London, Penguin, 2021) 152

the 1830s and 40s slowly killed off the intermingling of Indian and British ideas, religion and ways of life.[6]

My school history books used to crow about the merciful role that the West African Squadron of the British Navy played in stopping Portuguese, Spanish and U.S. ships taking slaves to the Americas after Britain had outlawed the slave trade. But David Olusoga reveals that "more recently historians have pointed out how the mission to end slavery dovetailed with suspicious ease into British colonial expansion in Africa, allowing British power and trade to penetrate into the region in the second half of the nineteenth century".[7]

During the sixty years of the reign of Queen Victoria, the British Empire had grown ten times, "from a scatter of disregarded possessions to a quarter of the land mass of the earth, and a third of its population".[8] As a wolf cub and then a boy scout, I took on board the outlook of Major-General Baden-Powell, the founder of the Scout movement and the author of *Scouting for Boys*. "I wish I had time to tell you the story of how we came to have this Empire," he wrote, "it is a wonderful tale of adventure and romance." Running that Empire required Britons prepared to move to the far-flung corners of the world. Baden-Powell in *Scouting for Boys* stressed the importance of colonial service but even more important were the writers of books for children who set out to make the imperial mission as thrilling as possible.

A rattling good yarn

I was brought up on such books myself and devoured them. An especial favourite was *Coral Island* about three boys who were castaway on a desert island. Re-reading it seventy years later I could understand the initial attraction—a life of "uninterrupted harmony and happiness".[9] The boys build their own boat and R.M. Ballantyne vividly describes their first voyage in it: "The sea was shining like a sheet of glass yet heaving with the long deep swell … and the bright sea-weeds and the brilliant corals shone in the depth of that pellucid water, as we rowed over it, like rare and precious gems." Even more exciting, the boys discover, by a prolonged dive, their very own secret cavern and discover its "deep intense stillness" and "the stupendous dome above and the countless gems that had sparkled in

6   William Dalrymple theguardian.com/uk/2002/dec/09/britishidentity.india
7   David Olusoga *Black and British—a forgotten history* (London, Macmillan, 2016) 298
8   James Morris *Heaven's Command—An Imperial Progress* (London, Penguin, 1973) 539
9   R.M.Ballantyne *Coral Island* (London, Dean and Son, no date given) 85

Baden-Powell in 1896, at the time of the Matabele campaign.

Coral Island—The three boys after shipwreck.

the torchlight." I was so thrilled by this description that I enrolled on a Youth Hostel Association course on underwater swimming and became Man Fish number 554.

But re-reading it seventy years later was a shock. Writing in 1857, Ballantyne consistently describes the indigenous people of the South Seas islands as "savages" who he sees as demonstrating their "natural depravity".[10] Early on in the book he refers to them as "wild, bloodthirsty savages, excepting in those favoured isles to which the gospel of our Saviour had been conveyed".[11] At one point, Peterkin, the leader of the three boys, spells out his agenda, all too close to Britain's imperialist policy at that time: "We've got an island all to ourselves. We'll take possession in the name of the king; we'll go and enter the service of its black inhabitants. Of course, we'll rise, naturally, to the top of affairs. White men always do in savage countries…".[12]

As well as Peterkin, *Coral Island* has another hero. Ralph, the novel's narrator, identifies him as "an English gentleman, who I at once and rightly concluded was a missionary … The expression of his countenance was the most winning I ever saw, and his clear blue eyes beamed with a look that was frank, fearless, loving and truthful". *Coral Island* was written at a time when the missionary Dr Livingstone was finding his way along the Zambezi river, naming one of its spectacular waterfalls the Victoria Falls and becoming a national hero. He was later described by Henry Morton Stanley, who famously tracked him down in Africa, as reverentially as the missionary is described in *Coral Island*; Stanley refers to him as being, though a man with defects, as "almost Christ-like for goodness, patience and self sacrifice".[13] This veneration for missionaries rubbed off on me during my childhood and for a few years I aspired to be one myself, perhaps hoping one day to win the commendation of *Coral Island*'s narrator—"God bless and prosper the missionaries till they get a footing in every island of the sea!"[14]

After Stanley's meeting with Livingstone, his American publisher cabled him: "YOU ARE NOW [AS] FAMOUS AS LIVINGSTONE HAVING DISCOVERED THE DISCOVERER".[15] Stanley described a later exploration, from the source of the Congo river to its mouth, "as an

10   Ballantyne,123
11   Ballantyne *Coral Island,* 6
12   Ballantyne, 12
13   Stanley *The Autobiography of Henry Morton Stanley* (London, Elibron Classics reprint of undated original) 295
14   Ballantyne, 121
15   Quoted by Tim Jeal in *Stanley* (London, Faber and Faber, 2007) 133

expedition organised solely for the purposes of exploration" contradicting that with the rest of his sentence "with a view to search out new avenues for commerce to the mutual advantages of civilisation and such strange lands as we found suitable for commercial and missionary enterprise".[16] After yet another African expedition, he was greeted by cheering crowds on his return to London and later became a Liberal Unionist MP.

Even at the time, there were some who were appalled by Stanley's initial defence of King Leopold of Belgium's brutally exploitative regime in the Congo. Shocked too by the bullying attitude to Africans revealed by his books, and what a black journalist the Rev. George Washington Williams, who visited the Congo in 1890, referred to as Stanley's "broken promises, his copious profanity, his hot temper, his heavy blows, his severe and rigorous measures, by which they [the people of the Congo] are mulcted of their lands".[17] Yet Stanley was knighted by Queen Victoria for his services to the British Empire, was widely perceived as a national hero, and a statue of him was erected in Denbigh in— astonishingly—2011!

Oh, for a Gatling!

A year after Stanley reached the mouth of the Congo river—1877—would-be novelist Henry Rider Haggard was raising the Union Jack to mark the British annexation of the Boer Republic of the Transvaal. He went on to write *King Solomon's Mines*, another of the adventure books that I relished in my boyhood and hugely popular throughout the Victorian era. How inspired I once was by the words of Sir Henry Curtis, the leader of the expedition to find the lost world of the goldmines, "…there is no journey upon this earth that a man may not make if he sets his heart on it," he tells his Zulu guide, "there is nothing, Umbopa, that he cannot do. There are no mountains he may not climb, there are no deserts he cannot cross…".[18]

My second reading, seventy years later, provided some shocks. As well as tales of derring-do, the book records with relish big-game hunting on a colossal scale. After shooting a young giraffe, the explorers move on to elephant extermination "eight elephants being a pretty good bag for one day".[19] Later death on the battlefield is described with equal relish and the narrator Alan Quatermain writes of the Kukuana tribe as "wonderful people. Death has no terrors for them when it incurred in the course of

16 Stanley *Through the Dark Continent* (London, Elibron Classics Replica Edition, 2006)
17 Quoted by John Hope Franklin in *George Washington Williams: A Biography* (Duke University Press, 1998)
18 Henry Rider Haggard *King Solomon's Mines* (London, Collins Classics, 2013) 48
19 Haggard, 42

"Look out! You drop that box, I'll shoot you". Stanley to a porter carrying Livingstone's journals— from a Stanley lantern lecture.

duty".[20] The reader gets a hint of the attitude that would later lead to the madness of the First World War when he refers to an inevitable death toll of an imminent battle: "It could not be otherwise; with that sagacious recklessness of human life which marks the great general, and often saves his forces and attains his ends, they were being condemned to inevitable slaughter, in order to give their cause and the remainder of the army a chance of success".[21]

The Wikipedia entry on Rider Haggard[22] seems inclined to exempt him from charges of racism on the grounds that he deplores the use of the term 'nigger'[23] but seems inclined to overlook his reference to 'Kaffirs' and 'savages'.[24] The entry also refers forgivingly to Haggard's mention of "women (black and white) who are smarter and emotionally stronger than men", but although his central character Quatermain hints at male desire for a black woman—"the soft-eyed, shapely Kukuana beauty"[25]—the same

20 Haggard, 155
21 Haggard, 158
22 En.wikipedia.org/wiki/Allan_Quatermain
23 Haggard, 5
24 Haggard, 36, 150, 163
25 Haggard, 178

"Fire you scoundrels". Illustration by Thure de Thulstrup for
King Solomon's Mines

woman articulates what is surely Haggard's own perspective "for the sun may not mate with the moon, nor the white with the black".[26]

Just before the battle scene in the novel, Captain Good, one of the white explorers, says wistfully, "Oh, for a Gatling!" adding, "I would clear that plain in twenty minutes".[27] The Gatling machine gun was invented in 1861, and in 1884, just a year before *King Solomon's Mines* was published, Stanley took a Maxim version of the machine gun with him, plus 30,000 cartridges, on another of his African expeditions. The gun became synonymous with imperial expansion and the Scramble for Africa. During Britain's war with the Matabele in 1893, the prolonged war in which Baden-Powell was later to make his name, it was claimed that the Maxim gun shot down 1,600 Matabele warriors[28] and so ensured victory. The poet Hilaire Belloc wrote a poem which included the lines:

26 Haggard, 204
27 Haggard,148
28 militaryhistorynow.com/2017/10/24/machine-gun-how-hiram-maxims-rapid-fire-invention-changed-history/

Whatever happens, we have got
The Maxim gun and they have not.

In 1893, Bristolian Harry Bow was excited to come across a Maxim gun—"real one they use in the performance"—in the vestibule of the Princes Theatre in Bristol, part of the promotion for a touring production of *A Life of Pleasure*. Harry was shrewd enough to realize what lay behind this plug for a play—"a terrible & deadly weapon capable of firing 600 shots a minute … and did terrible execution among the enemy and mows down like sheaves of corn".[29]

Yo-ho-ho and a bottle of rum

Apologists for Haggard and other imperialist writers sometimes argue that it is unfair to judge their output by the ethical criteria of a later age. But the work of Robert Louis Stevenson suggests that it was possible to write in the Victorian period but not to fall into line with the prevailing jingoistic spirit. I loved the book *Treasure Island* as a child and can still remember the terror I felt when, in *Kidnapped*, David Balfour reaches the top of a spiral staircase—and finds a terrifying drop awaiting him.

Returning to *Treasure Island* in my 80s, I find not only a story as gripping as when I first read it but also writing that never talks down to a juvenile audience. There is a dramatic and vivid awareness of sound— "nothing but the low wash of the ripple and the croaking of the crows in the wood"[30] as Jim Hawkins and his mother await the return of Black Dog; "the ship was talking, as sailors say, loudly, treading the innumerable ripples with an incessant weltering splash"[31] as Jim manages to get back on board the Hispaniola; and, "there was no sound but that of the distant breakers, mounting from all round and the chirp of countless insects in the brush"[32] as Jim finally sets out with Long John Silver to dig up the treasure.

The term 'savages'[33] only pops up in one of Jim's dreams and his encounter with the reality of a West Indies port is described sympathetically: "It was just at sundown when we cast anchor in a most beautiful land-locked gulf, and were immediately surrounded by boats full of Negroes, and Mexican Indians and half-bloods … The sight of so many good-humoured

29 Diaries of W. Harry Bow Bristol Archives, Ref 31416
30 Robert Louis Stephenson *Treasure Island* (London, Puffin Classics edition, 2015) 31
31 Stephenson, 197
32 Stephenson, 278
33 Stephenson, 59

Jim Hawkins hiding in an apple barrel on the Hispaniola.

faces (especially the blacks) the taste of the tropical fruits and, above all, the lights that began to shine in the town, made a most charming contrast to our dark and bloody sojourn on the island".[34]

In the later years of his life, Stevenson and his family went to live in Samoa where he came to identify with the situation of the islanders against what he saw as European and American exploitation. In 1894, shortly before he died, he addressed Samoan tribal chiefs: "there is but one way to defend Samoa. Hear it before it is too late ... occupy and use your country ... if you do not occupy and use your country, others will".[35] Stevenson died in 1895 just before the "orgy of self-satisfaction"[36] that marked the celebration of Queen Victoria's Diamond Jubilee in 1897. Lord Curzon, the Viceroy of India wrote, "There has never been anything so great in the world's history as the British Empire, so great an instrument for the good of humanity".[37]

Playing the Great Game

Rudyard Kipling was also able to see imperialism at first hand but was more ambiguous in his attitude to it. His experience in India as a journalist provided him with rich material for an audience of children as well as for adults. The *Just So Stories* which he made up for his daughter Josephine, who died from pneumonia aged seven, and *The Jungle Book* continue to charm the young now. His novel *Kim* rather less so; it tells the story of the orphaned son of white parents in India who becomes a child of the streets and eventually a secret agent for the British government. In it Kipling demonstrates a vivid awareness of the rich culture of India and a realization, as one of its characters puts it, that "The Sahibs [those of European descent] have not *all* this world's wisdom".[38]

But Kim is taught at an English school in India that "One must never forget that one is a Sahib, and that some day, when examinations are passed, one will command natives".[39] He becomes a very effective spy helping to defend British interests in northern India against its opponents especially Russia, what Kipling famously described as "the Great Game that never ceases day and night, throughout India".[40] Kipling reveals his own loyalties most blatantly in some of his poetry:

34 Stephenson 301
35 En.wikipedia.org/wiki/Robert Louis Stevenson
36 Lindqvist, 78
37 Quoted by Wade Davies in *Into the Silence* (London, Vintage, 2012) 43
38 Rudyard Kipling *Kim* (London, Macmillan, 1944) 274
39 Kipling *Kim*,177
40 Kipling *Kim*, 250

John Buchan, author of *Prester John*, who later became
Baron Tweedsmuir and Governor-General of Canada.

Take up the White Man's Burden—
Send forth the best ye breed—
Go bind your sons to exile
To serve your captives' need;
To wait in heavy harness
On fluttered folk and wild—
Your new-caught, sullen peoples,
Half sullen and half child.

It has been suggested that those lines were intended to be ironic but they are all too compatible with Kipling's friendship with Rhodes, the mining magnate who proclaimed, "The Native is to be treated as a child and denied franchise".[41] On the outbreak of the First World War, he took on the role of a recruiter for the British Army. Edward Said, the author of *Orientalism*, was in no doubt about the writer's perspective: "Kipling's White Men are quite prepared to go to war ... Behind the White Man's mask of amiable leadership there is always the express willingness to use force, to kill and be killed".[42]

When the great guns spoke

In 1906 Kipling wrote "The Children's Song" to mark Empire Day, which was instituted after Victoria's death, to mark her birthday. Its first verse ran:

Land of our birth we pledge to thee
Our love and toil in the years to be;
When we are grown and take our place
As men and women with our race.

He was an enthusiastic supporter both of the war against the Boers and of the First World War and, in 1914, he agreed to write propaganda for the Government. So too did another adventure story writer of that period, John Buchan, who also had a strong link to the British Empire. After serving as the private secretary to the High Commissioner for South Africa, he wrote *Prester John* in which the hero sets out to make his fortune in South Africa. The novel is permeated with racist terms—'bloodthirsty savages', 'Kaffir', 'native babbles'—and the hero refers to himself as "going into native country and away from civilisation" and "hemmed in by barbarism, and

41 Quoted by Gary Younge in 'Tear them all down' *The Guardian* 1 June 2021, p7
42 Edward Said *Orientalism* (London, Penguin, 2019) 226

Lord Kitchener inspecting Boy Scouts during the First World War.

cut off in a ghoulish land from the succour of my own kind".[43] None of this disturbed me when read it as a child; then I saw it as the way of the world.

Although Buchan's novel accords a certain amount of respect for Laputa, the man who is seen as the re-incarnation of Prester John and as having come out of "high stock", he is represented as an intimidating "big black brute". What is seen as "a crusade against the white man"[44] is dealt with when "the great guns spoke ... and white Africa drew breath again".[45] Buchan's fiction is disturbingly close to the reality of British imperialism in this period. In 1906 the Matabele people rose in revolt against British rule and the British South Africa Company called in British troops, including Baden-Powell who recorded that he was pleased to "have a go" against an enemy "without much capacity to inflict damage on trained soldiers." In the battle that ensued, Baden-Powell and his troops killed two hundred "natives" at the cost of one dead European.[46]

Joseph Conrad never wrote a book for children but his novel *Heart of Darkness* is a powerful demonstration of the ability of some writers to rise above the prejudices of their age. The Nigerian writer Chinua Achebe has

---

43   John Buchan *Prester John* (London, House of Stratus, 2001) 56-7
44   Buchan, 52
45   Buchan, 201
46   Baden-Powell *The Matabele Campaign* (London, 1897/1901) 63

criticised the book on the grounds that it depersonalises a part of the human race, but Achebe has in turn been criticised for assuming that Marlowe, the central character, is simply the voice of Conrad. The line, "Exterminate all the brutes", spoken in the *Heart of Darkness* by Kurtz, an administrator for the Belgian government in the Congo, becomes the title of a book by Sven Lindqvist. In it Lindqvist writes, "Conrad would have been able to set his story using any of the peoples of European culture. In practice, the whole of Europe acted according to the maxim 'Exterminate all the brutes'".[47]

A novel published in 1912 by American Edgar Rice Burroughs, *Tarzan of the Apes*, crudely attempted to justify the brutality:

> "What would you do, Tarzan?" asks a French officer. "They will try to kill us if they see us", replied Tarzan, "I prefer to be the killer." "Maybe they are friends", suggested D'Arnot. "They are black" was Tarzan's only reply.[48]

I read and enjoyed reading Tarzan books as a boy, unable to see the way that eugenicist Burroughs saw Tarzan as a demonstration of how, in spite of all impediments, breeding would manifest itself: "It was the hallmark of his aristocratic birth, the natural outcropping of many generations of fine breeding, an hereditary instinct of graciousness which a lifetime of uncouth and savage training and environment could not eradicate".[49]

As rival Empires clashed around the world, "boys adventure stories focussed upon links between manliness as a virtue and fighting, glamorising the adventure, heroism and honour to be gained from military service and promoting a sense of duty and patriotism." This is how Lois Bibbings summarises it, and she goes on to point out that these stories were supplemented by 'true' narratives about military heroes and "formed part of the 'myth of Empire'".[50] The link was made explicit in film of Lord Kitchener, labelled a hero for his crushing of a Sudanese rebellion in 1898 and of the Boers in 1902, inspecting a group of Boy Scouts alongside Baden-Powell, who had initially planned to call his youth movement the Imperial Scouts.[51] After the outbreak of the First World War, the Boy Scouts become part of the recruitment campaign, parading in 1914 for what the *Western Daily Press* described as a "Great Military demonstration for Empire Day".[52]

47 Sven Lindqvist *Exterminate All the Brutes* (Granta, London, 2018) 171
48 Edgar Rice Burroughs *Tarzan of the Apes* (London, Penguin Red Classics, 2008) 299
49 Burroughs *Tarzan of the Apes*, 236
50 Lois Bibbings *Telling Tales About Men* (Manchester, Manchester University Press, 2014) 90
51 Sanghera *Empireland*, 11
52 *Western Daily Press* 25 May 1914

Disillusion

Some saw the outcome of the First World War as a triumph: "The British emerged from the conflict with the most powerful army in the world, its navy supreme, its empire enhanced by a surge of colonial acquisitions that would not end until 1935, when it would finally reach its greatest geographical extent".[53] But the brutality and the colossal death rate of the 'war to end all wars' gradually led to a degree of disillusionment. Perhaps the first to have their illusions shattered were those Jamaicans who had volunteered to fight for King and Country: "Repeatedly in 1914 and 1915, the British Empire was portrayed in local newspapers and rallies in support of the war as an empire of emancipation, a commonwealth of justice, freedom and even equality."[54] Josiah Wedgewood MP revealed the harsh truth when advocating the use of black soldiers in European service: "because we do not want all the whites killed—to put it bluntly. To slow down the rate of killing of our men and to eke out the finest race on Earth".[55]

In the Victory Parade on 19th July 1919 black troops were totally excluded. "We can only conclude" wrote the *African Telegraph,* the newspaper of the Society of Peoples of African Origin, "that it is the policy of His Majesty's Ministers to ignore the services of the black subjects of the Empire".[56] De-mobilised British soldiers found out that Lloyd George's "land fit for heroes" was an empty promise and many of the conscientious objectors who had been imprisoned during the war now found they were getting a sympathetic hearing. Walter Ayles had spent most of the war in prison as a conscientious objector but when he was released in 1919 and stood again as a councillor for Easton ward in Bristol, he won comfortably with a majority of 400; according to the *Western Daily Press,* the crowd at Easton School "received the announcement with shouts of satisfaction".[57] By 1924 there were 15 MPs who had been COs elected to Parliament and a dinner was given in their honour in the House of Commons.[58]

The changed perspective had repercussions in youth movements after 1918. "On the issue of *militarism*", wrote Leslie Paul, "the pre-war record of the Scout movement was not a happy one".[59] In 1925 he founded the Woodcraft Folk, a democratic organisation for boys and girls, which looked

53 Wade Davies *Into the Silence,* 91
54 David Olusoga, *Black and British- a Forgotten History* (London, Macmillan, 2016) 429
55 Olusoga, 441
56 Quoted by Olusoga, 448
57 Colin Thomas, *Slaughter No Remedy* (Bristol, Bristol Radical History Group, 2017) 17
58 *Refusing To Kill* (Bristol, Bristol Radical History Group, 2018) 41
59 Leslie Paul *Angry Young Man* (London, Faber and Faber, undated) 55

"Bobbie still waved the flags". Illustration for
The Railway Children by C.E.Brock.

forward to a time "when man shall turn his labour from private greed to social service to increase the happiness of mankind, and when nations shall cease to suckle tribal enmities and unite in common fellowship".[60] In 1925 the Bristol Company Life Brigade were also keen to disassociate themselves from militarism: "Some people may imagine as they witness the Company on parade, that the drill savours of militarism and may inculcate the martial spirit. Let it be stated that the spirit of militarism has no place whatsoever in the movement ... the use of arms is entirely eliminated".[61]

The tone and style of children's books seemed to change post war too. Two of the most popular in that period were *The Railway Children* and *Swallows and Amazons,* both books in which girls had as important a role as boys: "Girls are just as clever as boys, and don't you forget it"[62] says the father in *The Railway Children.* That father is sent to prison unjustly and his wife, who holds the family together by her published writing, tells her three children "when you say your prayers, I think you might ask God to show His pity upon all prisons and captives".[63] Although the book was published before the War in 1906, its comparatively liberal outlook caught the mood of parents buying books for their children after 1918.

The book spells out the problems faced by the poor, made sharper because the family on which it is focussed had previously been comparatively well off—the fear of a doctor's bill now hangs over them as it did for most people at the time. Edith Nesbit, the author, was a Fabian and very aware of the risk of a patronising Lady Bountiful attitude to the poor: "charity's what I never did abide, and won't neither"[64] insists Perks the porter. The mother in the book ignores the station master's suspicious attitude to a Russian refugee—"I hope you won't find you're taking home a frozen viper"—and gives him shelter.[65]

What is most striking about both *The Railway Children* and *Swallows and Amazons* is the gently humorous style: both include writers struggling for opportunities to get on with their writing, sharply different from the blood-and-thunder of the children's (almost exclusively boys') books of the previous generation. *Swallows and Amazons* sends up the notion of a world arbitrarily divided between 'us' on the one hand and 'savages' and 'natives' on the other. 'Savages' are adults they don't know and 'natives' adults they

60   Quoted by Leslie Paul, 63
61   2nd Bristol Company Life Brigade Camp Magazine, August 1925
62   E. Nesbit *The Railway Children* (London, Puffin Books, 2010) 6
63   E. Nesbit, 101
64   E. Nesbit, 178
65   E. Nesbit, 96

Biggles on the cover of *The Modern Boy* magazine, 1934.

Timothy the dog saves the day, drawing by Eileen Soper, from *Five on a Treasure Island*.

do know. Alliances are meaningless: "But we want the sort of alliance that will let us fight each other if we want to";[66] and 'war' a state of mind: "We can't very well be at war with each other while we're living in the same camp".[67]

Arthur Ransome, the author of *Swallows and Amazons,* had been a foreign correspondent in Russia during the revolution where he met Trotsky's secretary who subsequently became his second wife. He got caught up in the intrigues and violent conflicts of that period and it is easy to understand why memories of his idyllic and privileged childhood (few children would have had ready access to a yacht) grew in significance for him. He later wrote of his much-loved book: "I could not help writing it. It almost wrote itself".[68]

Savage heart of a savage continent

But the success of Ransome and Nesbit didn't mean that the days of imperialist writing for children were over. Zooming out of a cloudless sky, guns blazing came Captain W.E. Johns, First World War pilot and creator of Biggles. His first book *The White Fokker* (pun intended?) published in 1932 uses the term 'Hun' throughout and the second *The Cruise of the Condor,* the N word appears four times. A Biggles website[69] says defensively "Of course in its day, the word was in regular use and not considered offensive at all"! It still appears, though in reported speech, in an edition of *The Cruise of the Condor* published in 1985.[70]

Racist attitudes permeate *The Cruise of the Condor*: "crazy natives", "wild tribes", "a treacherous lot" and, referring to South America, the "savage heart of a savage continent".[71] Biggles pines for the return of warfare: "This peace seems a grim business for me" and "there are times when I positively ache to hear a gun go off".[72] Biggles, who never seemed to age, had no difficulty in going into action during the Second World War and the Air Ministry gave his author W.E. Johns the job of creating a female version—Worral—to encourage recruitment into the WAAF. In 1941 the Boy Scouts movement, which had always been close to the armed forces,

66   Arthur Ransome *Swallows and Amazons* (London, Vintage Books, 2012) 148
67   Ransome, 331
68   Ransome, 504
69   http://www.biggles.info/Details/04/01/
70   W. E. Johns *Biggles and the Cruise of the Condor* (London, Deans International Publishing, 1985) 45, 158
71   Johns 17,19,25,39
72   Johns 7,8

initiated Air Scouts and the RAF later provided recognition including special opportunities and trips.[73]

In 1940, George Orwell turned his sharp eye on to writing for children, arguing that, "the worst books are often the most important, because they are usually the ones that are read earliest in life". The stories in the older boys' magazines like *Gem* and *Magnet*, he noted, are centred in posh public schools—"fantastically unlike life at a real public school", says Orwell—but read widely by boys who would never attend one. Orwell himself had been a pupil at Eton and for his 'Boys' Weeklies' essay conscientiously waded through more of what were then recent publications like *Skipper* and *Champion*. He concludes that in all of them "there is being pumped out in them the conviction that the major problems of our time do not exist, that there is nothing wrong with laissez-faire capitalism, that foreigners are unimportant comics, and the British Empire is a sort of charity-concern which will last for ever".[74]

Enid Blyton's popularity took off after the Second World War and she was spared Orwell's ruthless analysis. She imitated the boy/girl mix of *The Railway Children* and *Swallows and Amazons,* but the boys tend to get the leadership roles while the girls make the sandwiches. Upper-lips are mostly kept stiff: "Boys don't cry", says tomboy George, "Anyway, I've never seen one, and I always try not to cry myself".[75] She is persuaded to behave more like a girl: "They are making me more like I ought to be".[76]

My brothers and I read Enid Blyton books voraciously during our boyhood and seventy years later it is just about possible to understand why— apart from the very simple vocabulary—they had such appeal. Blyton is good at maintaining jeopardy, the-what-happened-next factor: just as they set off to row to the island (a treasure island of course), Julian takes the crucial map out of his pocket: "...and the wind at once blew it right out of his hands! It fell into the sea and bobbed there in the wind." The day is saved by the dog, the fifth member of the Famous Five: "He soon had the map in his mouth and was swimming back to the boat. The children thought he was simply marvellous!"[77]

Neither my brothers nor I were aware then of Blyton's sexism or racism. It wasn't until 1960 that Macmillan refused to publish Blyton's *The Mystery That Never Was* noting her "faint but unattractive touch of old-fashioned

73 Wikipedia.org/wiki/Air_Scout
74 George Orwell 'Boys' Weeklies' in *Inside the Whale and Other Essays* 1940
75 Enid Blyton *Five on a Treasure Island* (London, Hodder and Stoughton, 1997) 26
76 Blyton, 107
77 Blyton, 108

xenophobia"; and the subtext of *The Little Black Doll* was painfully obvious: Sambo is ostracised for his "ugly black face" accepted only when his face is washed "clean" by the rain.[78]

But publisher William Collins snapped up *The Mystery That Never Was* knowing that the name Enid Blyton meant huge sales. To many parents, my own included, what really mattered was that Blyton's clever story-telling technique—the page-turning factor—persuaded children to read and keep reading. I can recall in retrospect my own local library in Cardiff hinting at its own disapproval of Enid Blyton but nevertheless making available, even encouraging, 'classic' children's books like *Coral Island, King Solomon's Mines* and *Prester John*. And at my grammar school every year we celebrated Empire Day, until in 1957 a handful of sixth formers refused to attend. Our headmaster shrugged his shoulders, "if you don't want to be there, you don't have to."

Wider still and wider

It was a Tory PM Harold Macmillan who coined the phrase "the wind of change", in relation to what was beginning to happen within the British Empire, but hardly a breath of it reached libraries and bookshelves. Even the more enlightened children's comics, like the *Eagle,* serialised comic strips about the lives of imperial heroes such as Rhodes and Livingstone. Sathnam Sanghera in his book *Empireland* asserts that "…right into the 1950s, the British were portrayed with an imperial bent in novels and publications especially those aimed at the young…".[79]

But in the 1950s a different kind of children's fiction emerged: the other worldliness of C.S. Lewis and J.R. Tolkien, and later that of J.K. Rowling's Harry Potter books. Lewis's Narnia books have a strong Christian subtext, and some have seen in Tolkien an implied racism: "…Tolkien's good guys are white", wrote Stephen Shapiro, "and the bad guys are black, slant-eyed, unattractive, inarticulate and a psychologically undeveloped horde".[80] My own children responded more to the mischievous subversion of Roald Dahl, books like *Danny Champion of the World*. Mr Hazell the local landowner and "Dukes and lords, barons and baronets, wealthy businessmen and all the fancy folk in the county"[81] get their come-uppance when Danny and his father manage to disrupt

78 theguardian.com/books/2021/jun/17/english-heritage-racism-kipling-blyton-blue-plaques
79 Sanghera, *Empireland*, 175-6
80 rediff.com/news/2003/jan/08lord.htm
81 Roald Dahl *Danny Champion of the World* (London, Puffin Books, 2001) 94

their annual pheasant shoot by drugging the intended victims. Part of Dahl's appeal to children is the discomfort he gives parent-readers who would be horrified by the idea of their child driving a car on their own at night, a key moment in the story.

Sometimes it is more than discomfort. Fat Augustus Gloop, "this greedy brute, this louse's ear",[82] gets duly punished for his greed in *Charlie and the Chocolate Factory* and Dahl apparently had to be persuaded out of making the Oompah Loompahs, the Chocolate Factory's workforce, pygmies rescued by Willie Wonka from "the very deepest and darkest part of the African jungle where no white man had been before".[83] Only when the book was to be filmed was Dahl persuaded to make changes to the book, however, the author continued to be blatantly outspoken about his anti-semitism.[84]

Dahl's popularity was enhanced by the films made from his books and then by the televising of those films. Willie Wonka would not have approved. As he saw it, television:

…rots the senses in the head!
It kills imagination dead!
It clogs and clutters up the mind!
It makes a child so dull and blind
He can no longer understand
A fantasy, a fairyland!

Willie Wonka—and surely Dahl too—pined for the time when children read books

And once they start—oh boy, oh boy!
You watch the slowly growing joy…[85]

The Letterbox Library launched in the 1980s was equally keen to encourage children to read but not *any* book: "We specialise in books in which children can see themselves and which reflect our world community in all its diversity".[86] Dahl's books did not appear in the Library's list and don't now. It wasn't enough for a book to be anti-racist: "inclusive content

82   Roald Dahl *Charlie and the Chocolate Factory* (London, Puffin Books, 2005) 105
83   Daily.jstor.org/roald-dahls-anti-black-racism
84   time.com/5937507/roald-dahl-anti-semitism
85   Dahl *Charlie and the Chocolate Factory* 172, 174
86   Letterboxlibrary.com

NOUGHTS & CROSSES

MALORIE BLACKMAN

'THE NOUGHTS & CROSSES SERIES ARE MY FAVOURITE BOOKS OF ALL TIME' STORMZY

Original cover design by Fruzsina Czech.

is not enough; our reviewers only select books which show excellence in storyline/artwork."

J.K. Rowling does make it in the Letterbox Library but only as part of the *Anthology of Amazing Women*. The anthology argues that her Harry Potter books weren't "just about magic; it reflected real people and real things".[87] Bizarrely, Rowling puts her characters into a boarding school environment although, as with the *Gem* and *Magnet* followers that Orwell analysed, few of her readers would have experienced one. Rowling does attempt to raise the issue of racism in an oblique way in her children's books, referring to the attempt by Voldemort, the villain of the Harry Potter series, to ensure the "purification of the wizarding race, getting rid of Muggle-borns and having pure bloods in charge".[88] 'Muggle-borns' are those not born of wizard parents, referred to negatively as "Mudbloods"; those who use the term are censured for doing so: "'Don't call her a Mudblood!' said Ron and Ginny together, very angrily".[89]

But all this is very confusing to a reader not familiar with the Harry Potter universe. The analogy used by Malorie Blackman in her *Noughts and Crosses* novels for young adults is clearer and sharper. She creates a world in which black people—Crosses—are dominant, treating white people—Noughts—as inferior. There is a clear reference to imperialism: "'…we have been the dominant race on Earth', a Cross teacher tells a history class. 'We have been the explorers, the ones to move entire backward civilisations onwards…'".[90]

Culture wars

In 2021 the Runnymede Trust together with Penguin Books produced the 'Lit in Colour' report, highlighting the fact that 82% of young people surveyed didn't recall ever studying a text by a Black, Asian or minority ethnic author. "It is vital" said the report, "that the books we read reflect the rich diversity of the society we live in".[91] Even the ever-popular children's comics woke up to a changing age. In the *Beano* comic 'Screwtop Science', 'Har Har's Joke Shop' and 'The Chandras'—"Meet Beanotown's Funniest Family"—all feature BAME characters portrayed sympathetically, and Freddie is now no longer Fatty and Walter has ceased to be Softy.[92]

87   Sandra Lawrence *Anthology of Amazing Women* (London, Templar Books, 2018) 104
88   J.K.Rowling *Harry Potter and the Order of the Universe* (London, Bloomsbury, 2014) 103
89   J.K.Rowling 99
90   Malorie Blackman *Noughts & Crosses* (London, Penguin Books, 2003) 130
91   Litincolour.penguin.co.uk
92   *Beano,* 2 July 2021

These kinds of developments set off a predictable response from the unwoke. Early in his tenure as Secretary of State for Education, Michael Gove announced that history lessons in schools should "celebrate" the legacy of the British Empire. When the BBC considered dropping 'Land of Hope and Glory' from the last night of the Proms, some expressed outrage. The BBC succumbed and yet again the chorus echoed around the Royal Albert Hall:

Wider still and wider
Shall thy bounds be set
God who made thee mighty
Make thee mightier yet.

At the same time the British Army was making sure that its recruitment in British schools continued unrestrained; only in Britain are 16-year-olds allowed to enlist, elsewhere in Europe they have to be 18. Forces Watch has drawn attention to the British Army's Militarisation Offensive of 2006 which encouraged "the promotion of the 'military ethos' in schools (including the Cadet Force) together with increasing the visibility of the military domestically".[93] Meanwhile Michael Gove was pushing for a pro-Empire orientation in school's history teaching, claiming that "too much history is informed by post-colonial guilt".[94]

More recently, the former Tory Culture Secretary Oliver Dowden has been leaning on British Museums to move away from what he describes as "a position of guilt and shame or the denigration of this country's past".[95] Hearteningly it seems that this pronouncement is likely to meet resistance: the collection that Bristol Museum inherited from the defunct British Empire and Commonwealth Museum "contains evidence of the violent oppression of black and brown people across the world" writes Lauren MacCarthy in a Bristol Museum blog, "as well as the sustained exploitation of communities and the environment. It also contains stories of hope and courage, creativity and environment".[96]

Stories about the past, whether fictional or factual, should aspire to tell the whole truth, including that of the all too often Brutish Empire.

Colin Thomas

93 Paul Dixon *Warrior Nation, militarism and British democracy* (Forces Watch 2018) forceswatch.net/wp-content/uploads/Warrior_Nation_web-1.pdf
94 Quoted in tes.com/news/British-empire-isn't-fantasy-villain-history-teaching-study-finds
95 *Daily Mail*, 7 July 2021
96 Lauren MacCarthy blog, 15 June 2020

Bibliography

Non-fiction

Bibbings, Lois, *Telling Tales About Men*. Manchester University Press, 2014

Evans, Chris, *Slave Wales*. University of Wales Press, 2010

Jeal, Tim, *Stanley*. Faber and Faber, 2007

Olusoga, David, *Black and British, a Forgotten History*. Macmillan, 2016

Said, Edward, *Orientalism*. Penguin, 2003

Sanghera, Sathnam, *Empireland*. Penguin, 2021

Fiction

Ballantyne R.M., *Coral Island*. Puffin Classics, 1994

Blackman, Malorie, *Noughts and Crosses*. Penguin, 2003

Blyton, Enid, *Five on a Treasure Island*. Hodder and Stoughton, 1997

Buchan, John, *Prester John*. Birlinn General, 2020

Burroughs, Edgar Rice, *Tarzan of the Apes*. Penguin Classics, 2008

Dahl, Roald, *Danny Champion of the World*. Puffin Books, 2001

Dahl, Roald, *Charlie and the Chocolate Factory*. Puffin Books, 2005

Johns, W.E., *Biggles and the Curse of the Condor*. Dean Publishing, 1985

Kipling, *Rudyard, Kim*. Wordsworth Classics, 1994

Nesbitt, Edith, *The Railway Children*. Puffin Books, 2010

Ransome, Arthur, *Swallows and Amazons*. Vintage Books, 2017

Rider Haggard, H., *King Solomon's Mines*. Collins Classics, 2013

Rowling, J.K., *Harry Potter and the Order of the Universe*. Bloomsbury, 2014

Stevenson, Robert Louis, *Treasure Island*. Puffin Classics, 2015

Picture Credits

Page 5—Robert Baden-Powell by Francis Henry Hart, for Elliott & Fry albumen cabinet card, 1896. National Portrait Gallery.

Page 6 —Illustration by The Brothers Dalziel, from *The Coral Island* by R. M. Ballantyne, Nelson edition. Wikicommons and Gutenberg.org.

Page 9—From *How I found Livingstone: travels, adventures, and discoveries in Central Africa, including four months' residence with Dr. Livingstone* by Henry M. Stanley. Archive.org.

Page 10—Illustration by Thure de Thulstrup, from *Maiwa's Revenge* by H. Rider Haggard. Wikicommons.

Page 12—Illustration by George Roux, from *Treasure Island* by Robert Louis Stevenson, Cassell edition, 1885. Wikicommons.

Page 14— John Buchan, 1st Baron Tweedsmuir by Bassano Ltd., 1935. National Portrait Gallery.

Page 16—*Boy Scouts Inspected AKA Lord Kitchener 1914-1918*. British Pathé.

Page 19—Illustration by C. E. Brock, from *The Railway Children* by E. Nesbit.

Page 21—Cover of *The Modern Boy magazine*, Issue 324, 1934.

Page 22—Illustration by Eileen A. Soper, from *Five on a Treasure Island* by Enid Blyton. Archive.org.

Page 27—Cover by Fruzsina Czech, from *Noughts and Crosses* by Malorie Blackman, Penguin Random House.

Acknowledgements

Thanks to Hazel Gower and to those Bristol Radical History members—Trish Mensah, Barbara Segal, Silu Pascoe—who read early drafts of Indoctrinating for Empire and offered helpful advice. Especial thanks to Richard Grove for his excellent graphic work and to Richard Musgrove who steered the project and provided wise guidance throughout.

The Kitchener and Boy Scouts photo was supplied by British Pathé and the author much appreciated the positive response he received from Fruzsi Czech, whose powerful cover for Noughts and Crosses is included in the pamphlet.